BIRD BRAINIACS

Activity journal and log book for young birders.

By Stacy Tornio and Ken Keffer

Illustrated by Rachel Riordan

BIRD BRAINIACS

Activity journal and log book for young birders.

First Hardcover Edition published in 2016

ISBN: 978-1-943645-47-3

Printed in USA

10 9 8 7 6 5 4 3 2 1

Book design by Patricia Gonzalez
Edited by Kristen Cianni and Brian Scott Sockin

Produced by the
Cornell Lab Publishing Group
Imprint of Wundermill, Inc.
321 Glen Echo Ln., Ste. C
Cary, NC 27518

www.CornellLabpg.com

DEDICATION PAGE

This is your book. You're going to fill the pages with your bird sightings, observations, artwork, and doodles. So go ahead and dedicate this book to a special bird person in your life!

I dedicate this book to ______________________________

HOW TO USE THIS JOURNAL

Write in it. Draw in it. Share it with friends. This book is really what YOU make of it. It's definitely a place where you can record your bird sightings—the bird log section starts on page 62—but it's a lot more than that too.

Take it along on a trip, and try out the games. Share it with a friend, and compare answers. Keep it throughout the year to write down the birds you see. And finally, hold onto it for years to come, because your love of birds isn't going to go away. It'll be fun to look back on it as you get older and experience more great bird moments.

CONTENTS

FILL IN THE BLANKS

ALL ABOUT ME

This journal truly is all about you! Fill out all the answers, and then compare them with your friend's or your sibling's answers. It's always fun to get to know one another better!

My name:

My siblings:

My parents:

My pets:

My best friend:

My favorite part of nature:

My hobbies:

Where I live:

FAVORITE

color:	food:	book:	movie:

FAVORITE	teacher:	animal:
FAVORITE	vacation spot:	season:
FAVORITE	holiday:	place to go hiking:
FAVORITE	bird:	place to watch birds:

Other things I want people to know about me:

TheCornellLab

BIRD Facts

WOOD DUCKS

The Wood Duck is one of the only ducks in North America that nests in tree cavities or nest boxes.

Wood Ducks can produce multiple broods of eggs in a single year.

Wood Duck

QUIZ

WHICH BIRD WOULD YOU RATHER BE?

It's a "Would You Rather?" questionnaire in the style of birds! Think hard about your options before answering!

1. An American Crow or a Common Raven?
2. A Ruby-throated Hummingbird or a Rufous Hummingbird?
3. A Great Horned Owl or a Great Gray Owl?
4. A Bald Eagle or a Golden Eagle?
5. A Black-and-white Warbler or a Yellow Warbler?
6. An Eastern Bluebird or a Mountain Bluebird?
7. A Baltimore Oriole or a Scarlet Tanager?
8. A Harlequin Duck or a Long-Tailed Duck?
9. A Trumpeter Swan or a Canada Goose?
10. A Great Egret or a Great Blue Heron?
11. A Killdeer or an American Woodcock?
12. A Black-capped Chickadee or a Red-breasted Nuthatch?

13 A Tree Swallow or a Purple Martin?

14 A Northern Cardinal or a Mourning Dove?

15 A Pileated Woodpecker or a Northern Flicker?

16 A Wood Thrush or an American Robin?

17 A Yellow-billed Cuckoo or a Northern Shrike?

18 A Belted Kingfisher or a Roseate Spoonbill?

19 A Sandhill Crane or a Whooping Crane?

20 A Wild Turkey or a Greater Sage-Grouse?

The Cornell Lab

BIRD Facts

SWANS

Swans are known for mating for life; pairs will stay together for many years.

The Trumpeter Swan can stretch to be 6 feet long!

Trumpeter Swan

HOW WELL DO YOU KNOW OWLS?

Owls are some of the most intriguing birds out there, and they really are quite amazing. Test your knowledge about these cool birds. Answers are on page 94.

1. How much can owls swivel their heads around?

A *90°* **B** *180°* **C** *270°* **D** *360°*

2. Which of these owls will use a nest box in the backyard?

A *Great Horned Owl*

B *Burrowing Owl*

C *Northern Hawk Owl*

D *Eastern Screech-Owl*

3. While most owls only have a few young at a time, which species can have more than a dozen?

A *Great Horned Owl* **B** *Barn Owl*

C *Western Screech-Owl* **D** *Elf Owl*

4. After they eat, owls cough up a little ball of materials that they can't digest, including bones, fur, or insect exoskeletons. What is this called?

A *A pellet* **B** *A pill*

C *An owl ball* **D** *A cornball*

5. The objects on a Great Horned Owl that many people think are ears are called what?

A *Fake ears* **B** *Tufts*

C *Faux fur* **D** *Owl lobes*

6. Which owl has the largest wingspan in North America?

A *Great Gray Owl* **B** *Great Horned Owl*

C *Barred Owl* **D** *Boreal Owl*

7. Although many owls hunt at night, this one will hunt during the day.

A *Eastern Screech-Owl* **B** *Great Horned Owl*

C *Northern Saw-whet Owl* **D** *Snowy Owl*

8. Roughly how many different species of owls exist in the world?

A *50* **B** *100* **C** *200* **D** *400*

BIRD Facts

GREAT HORNED OWLS

The female Great Horned Owl is bigger than the male.

Large owls are fierce predators and will even go after other owls and raptors.

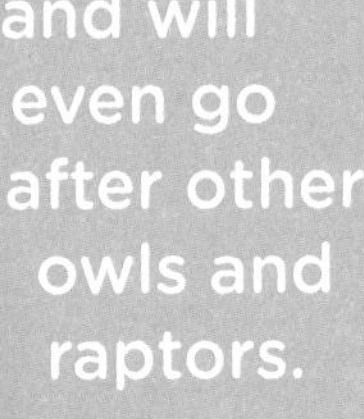

Great Horned Owl

NATURE TRUTH OR DARE

Here's a friendly game of Truth or Dare.
Grab a few friends and ask them to play!

TRUTH QUESTIONS

Is it true you're a bird nerd?

YES NO

Give an example of just how much you love birds.

Have you ever lied about seeing a bird when you really didn't?

YES NO

If you could make one person in your life like birds (who currently doesn't), who would it be and why?

Have you ever thrown garbage down outside?

YES NO

Is it true you've peed outside before?

YES NO

Is it true you're scared of the dark?

YES NO

Is it true you really like all birds?

YES NO

Name a bird you do not like.

Do you keep a bird list?

YES NO

How many species are on it?

If you could see only one bird for the rest of your life, what would it be and why?

Do you have any bird stuffed animals?

YES NO

What are they?

DARE QUESTIONS

- Flap your arms like a hummingbird for 30 seconds.
- Spin around 10 times, and then put your binoculars up to your eyes. What's the first thing you see?*
- Find bird poop outside. Then take a selfie with it.
- Make up a bird song that rhymes, and then sing it loudly.
- Hoot like a Great Horned Owl.
- Pick up as much trash as you can outside for 1 minute.
- Name as many birds that start with the letter S as you can in 15 seconds.
- Give yourself a temporary bird tattoo with a non-toxic pen or marker.
- Jump up in a crowded area and shout "I love birds" three times.
- Turn your shirt around backward and wear your binoculars backward for 5 minutes, too. See if you get any funny looks. (You will.)

** Make sure you have someone there to catch you in case you get dizzy!*

BIRD Facts

SANDHILL CRANES

When nesting, Sandhill Cranes are pretty territorial, and you'll only see a couple together at a time—sometimes more if they have young. However, during winter and migration, they will flock together in groups of thousands.

Look for cranes in fields, along water, or in marshes. In the fields, they'll be looking for grain to eat, and in the marshes, they'll be foraging for invertebrates.

Sandhill Crane

THE POWER OF Merlin®

Spending more time looking at birds is one way to improve your birding skills, but it's not the only way. Study up using the Cornell Lab's free Merlin Bird ID app. (Psst! It can also help you ID a mystery bird!)

Use the 5 questions Merlin will ask you to practice gathering information for the app.

1. Where did you see it?

   ____

2. When did you see it?

   ____

3. What was the size?

   ____

4. What was the color?

   ____

5. What activity was the bird doing?

   ____

Now take these data from a recent bird sighting, and go test out Merlin.

Don't forget to record your sightings. If you created an eBird account for your bird count, make sure to submit your checklist.

That helps others explore what's been seen in your area.

Mourning Dove

BIRD Facts

MOURNING DOVES

The oldest known Mourning Dove was 31 years 4 months old.

Mourning Doves are the most widespread and abundant gamebird in North America.

THINK QUICK

This is a fun game where there's truly no right or wrong answer. You simply write down the first thing or things you think of when you see the word or phrase. Your answers may or may not be bird-related; you just never know!

BALD EAGLE:

HUMMINGBIRDS:

FEEDING BIRDS:

BIRDS IN SPRING:

BIRDS IN SUMMER:

BABY BIRDS:

BLUEBIRDS:

BINOCULARS:

OWLS:

SUET:

BIRDS IN WINTER:

WOODPECKERS:

COMMON LOON:

MOUNTAIN BIRD:

TINY BIRD:

LARGE BIRD:

GREAT SWIMMER:

SPOTTED BIRD:

BIRDS IN FALL:

BEACH BIRD:

FUNNY BIRD:

NESTING:

COLORFUL BIRD:

EXOTIC BIRD:

TheCornellLab

BIRD Facts

BALD EAGLES

Young Bald Eagles look similar to Golden Eagles because it takes them five years to get their full white head and tail.

The wingspan of a Bald Eagle can be more than 7 feet.

Bald Eagle

QUIZ

TWO TRUTHS & A LIE

Can you figure out which of the following statements are lies? Put a "T" next to the two answers you think are true and an "F" next to the one you think is false. *Answers are on page 94.*

BIRD POOP

- ☐ Scat is another word for poop.
- ☐ Dubs is another word for poop.
- ☐ Turd is another word for poop.

DUCKS

- ☐ All ducks quack.
- ☐ Male ducks are called drakes.
- ☐ Ducks are divided into two main groups—divers and dabblers.

FEEDING

- ☐ Some birds will chew up insects and spit them back up to feed their babies.
- ☐ You shouldn't feed birds in fall because it'll keep them from migrating.
- ☐ Hummingbirds can eat 2,000 insects in a single day.

CROWS

- ☐ There is more than one species of crow in North America.
- ☐ Ravens are just bigger crows.
- ☐ Juvenile crows will help their parents feed their younger siblings.

ORIOLES

- ☐ Oriole nests are woven and they hang down like a sock.
- ☐ These birds will eat grape jelly and oranges.
- ☐ Orioles turn red when they fly south for winter.

WARBLERS

- [ ] You can find more than 100 warbler species in North America.
- [ ] The Yellow-rumped Warbler has a nickname of butterbutt.
- [ ] Most warblers eat insects, but a few will eat berries, especially in winter.

BIRDHOUSES

- [ ] Woodpeckers will use birdhouses or tree cavities.
- [ ] There are no species of owl that will use a nest box.
- [ ] Bluebirds like to have their nest box facing an open field.

HUMMINGBIRDS

- [ ] Hummingbirds are one of the only birds in the world that can fly backward.
- [ ] Hummingbirds lap up nectar, kind of like a dog.
- [ ] Hummingbirds have eggs the size of quarters.

TheCornellLab

BIRD Facts

PELICANS

Pelicans have the ability to incubate their eggs with their feet.

Have you ever seen a pelican eat? Brown Pelicans will dive into the water to scoop up a fish. Be on the lookout; it's fun to watch.

Every single continent in the world has pelicans on it—except Antarctica.

Brown Pelican

FILL IN THE BLANKS

BIRDING WISH LIST

When you have any hobby, it's always fun to dream big. Birding is no exception. Sure, it's always fun to notice and watch the birds in your own backyard, but what else is on your wish list? ***It's time to do a little daydreaming!***

My favorite bird sighting so far:

A bird I haven't seen but want to:

My favorite destination to see birds:

An exotic bird I want to see and why:

A destination I want to visit one day to see birds:

If I went to Alaska, I would want to see this bird:

If I went to Hawaii, I would want to see this bird:

Three places outside of North America where I want to see birds:

1

2

3

Three people I would take with me to see these birds:

1

2

3

Other animals I want to look for when searching for birds:

This bird took me a long time to see:

Here's where I finally saw this difficult-to-find bird:

More of my bird wishes and dreams:

TheCornellLab

BIRD Facts

GREEN JAYS

The only place you can find a Green Jay in the United States is in southern Texas.

Other jays in North America include the Blue Jay, Steller's Jay, and Florida Scrub-Jay, among others.

Green Jay

TRY A NestWatch EXPERIMENT

Have you ever participated in citizen science? *This just means that you've helped out scientists by writing down observations and information. Watching a nest is an easy way to be a citizen scientist, and it's really fun, too. Get involved in the Cornell Lab's NestWatch citizen-science program in just 5 easy steps!*

1

GET CERTIFIED. Register at nestwatch.org. Then you can become a certified NestWatcher by using the online resources and tests.

Why do you want to be a NestWatcher?

___

SEARCH. Use your new skills to find active nests to monitor.

What birds nest in your backyard or area?

___

___

3

VISIT NESTS. Check on the nests every 3 or 4 days. Be sure to record what you see.

What nest(s) do you want to find?

___

___

REPORT DATA. Use the Cornell Lab's forms to report your data online.

What do you think you'll find out about the nest you observe?

___

BE A BIRD NEST AMBASSADOR. You can do this step anytime. Help spread the word that nesting birds are fun to learn about and important to monitor.

What will you share and with whom are you going to share?

___

___

___

COMMON NESTWATCH SPECIES

- Eastern Bluebird
- Black-capped Chickadee
- House Wren
- Tree Swallow
- American Robin
- Northern Cardinal
- Eastern Phoebe
- Northern Mockingbird

TheCornellLab

BIRD Facts

BLUEBIRDS

Bluebirds don't have the right bill to dig out their own nesting cavities, so they look for woodpecker holes or other cavities to raise their young.

You can put out mealworms to help bluebirds feed their young.

Western Bluebird

WHAT'S FOR DINNER?

How well do you know what birds eat? Test your skills at this game by drawing a line from the bird to the food listed at the bottom. Some birds could have more than one answer but try to guess the best answer for each one. *See how you did on page 94.*

PLANT TUBERS | MEALWORMS | RABBIT | ROADKILL | SNAKE | NECTAR

BLACK-CAPPED
CHICKADEE

ROSEATE
SPOONBILL

SHRIMP

GNATS

CRACKED CORN

BLACK-OIL SUNFLOWER SEED

TheCornellLab

BIRD Facts

ROSEATE SPOONBILLS

The bill on a Roseate Spoonbill does serve a purpose. It actually filters food like aquatic invertebrates and small fish for spoonbills to eat.

Many people will think they're seeing a flamingo when they first spot a Roseate Spoonbill.

ARE YOU A NATURE PRO?

Put your bravery to the test in this fun quiz. Circle which description best describes you, and then flip to page 94 to see how you fared.

You see a snake slither behind a rock. Do you...

A. Hurry over to get a closer look?

B. Watch curiously from a distance?

C. Run in the other direction?

A bird lands on your head. What do you do?

A. Try to catch it so you can study it.

B. Hold still, hoping it will fly away soon.

C. Shriek and flail your arms all about.

If you see a box turtle in the middle of the road, what would you do?

A. Move it right away, and then get a closer look at it.

B. Get a glove or stick to help move it.

C. Ask someone else to move it for you.

When you catch a fish, what do you do?

A. Take it off the hook.

B. Put on a glove and try to take it off.

C. Have someone else take it off for you.

If you see a frog, do you...

A. Catch and study it right away?

B. Catch it, even if it takes a few attempts?

C. Put a bucket over it because you don't want to touch it? Ewww!

If you get bird poop on you, what do you do?

A. Laugh, and take a picture.

B. Complain about it, but not really mind it.

C. Shriek and get rid of it ASAP!

BIRD Facts

DOUBLE-CRESTED CORMORANTS

The double crests on the cormorant are only visible during the breeding season, and even then they can be difficult to see.

Cormorants often stand in the sun with their wings spread out.

Double-crested Cormorant

BIRD ADVENTURES IN THE SOUTHWEST

This bird story is meant to be fun and entertaining. Just ask a family member or friend to fill in the missing blanks. Then when you're all done, read the story out loud to see how unusual or bizarre it ended up.

Jamie put on his ________________ (*article of clothing*), and then put his ____________ (*color*) binoculars around his neck. "________________________ (*a phrase of excitement*)!" he said. "I'm ready to go find one of those _____________________ (*adjective*) roadrunners. They don't have roadrunners where I'm from in _______________________ (*state*)."

Jamie started ___________________ (*verb ending in ing*) down the ________________ (*object found in nature*) path in search of a roadrunner with his friends ___________________________ (*person*) and ____________________________ (*person*).

Jamie stopped at a _____________________ (*adjective*) group of trees. He didn't see a roadrunner, but he did see a __________________________ (*bird*) and a ___________________________ (*bird*) singing to one another.

Jamie cleared his ____________________ (*body part*) and started joining in the

singing by belting out his favorite song,

______________________________.
song

His friend tapped him on the

___________________________. "Look!
body part

There goes our roadrunner."

They all took off ______________________.
verb ending in ing

"This is going to be better than seeing a

__________________________," Jamie said.
bird

They ______________ as fast as they could,
verb

but they couldn't catch the roadrunner.

"Are you ______________________, Jamie?"
a feeling

his friend asked.

"______________________," he said.
another way to say no

"It just gives me an excuse to come

back tomorrow."

TheCornellLab

BIRD Facts

GREATER ROADRUNNERS

Greater Roadrunners can reach speeds over 18 miles an hour.

They will eat things like snakes, scorpions, frogs, or any other small animals.

Greater Roadrunner

BIRD MNEMONICS

Bird songs can be tough to learn, so sometimes you need to have a few tricks to help you remember what sounds each bird makes. This is where bird mnemonics can help! Draw a line to connect each bird name with its right bird song. Answers are on page 95.

"Drink your tea."

"Peter, Peter, Peter."

"Who cooks for you? Who cooks for you all?"

Tufted Titmouse

Barred Owl

Eastern Towhee

"Sweet, sweet, sweet. I'm so sweet."

"Oh sweet Canada, Canada, Canada."

"I gotta go wee wee right now."

Yellow Warbler

White-throated Sparrow

Black-capped Chickadee

White-crowned Sparrow

BIRD Facts

YELLOW WARBLERS

Like many warblers, Yellow Warblers will spend most of their day eating insects.

Brown-headed Cowbirds will often lay their eggs in a Yellow Warbler's nest.

Yellow Warbler

FILL IN THE BLANKS

SPARK BIRDS

In the birding world, a "spark bird" is a BIG DEAL—it's the bird that got you excited about birding for the first time. What was your "spark bird"? Share your story below.

My SPARK bird:

The story behind my SPARK bird:

FIVE other birds that have had a big influence on me:

1 ________ 2 ________ 3 ________

4 ________ 5 ________

My SPARK birding person (who was responsible for getting me to like birds):

My SPARK birding place:

When I want other people to like birds, I tell them about these three cool birds:

1 ______________ 2 ______________

3 ______________

My favorite time of year for birds and why:

Here's another SPARK moment I had in nature:

TheCornellLab

BIRD Facts

HUMMINGBIRDS

Hummingbirds can beat their wings over 50 times per second.

The Rufous Hummingbird is the only hummingbird that nests in Alaska.

Rufous Hummingbird

GROSS or GREAT

Circle whether you think the following items are gross (ewww!) or great (awesome!).

Bird feathers

EWWW! AWESOME!

Baby birds without feathers

EWWW! AWESOME!

Mom birds regurgitating into babies' mouths

EWWW! AWESOME!

An owl eating a rabbit

EWWW! AWESOME!

A loon catching a fish

EWWW! AWESOME!

A partially eaten bird in the backyard EWWW! AWESOME!

House Finches with an eye disease EWWW! AWESOME!

A hawk killing a mouse

EWWW! AWESOME!

Vultures eating roadkill

EWWW! AWESOME!

The bald head of a California Condor

EWWW! AWESOME!

Owl pellet

EWWW! AWESOME!

Birds pooping while flying

EWWW! AWESOME!

The beard on a Wild Turkey

EWWW! AWESOME!

Bird poop

EWWW! AWESOME!

An American Robin pulling a worm out of the ground

EWWW! AWESOME!

A mother bird carrying away fecal sacs from the nest

EWWW! AWESOME!

BIRD Facts

TURKEY VULTURES

Turkey Vultures have an amazing sense of smell. This is why they are such good scavengers of dead animals.

If vultures get scared (like if you were approaching them), they might vomit.

Vultures sometimes poop on their legs to help keep themselves from getting too hot.

Turkey Vulture

A picnic with THE BIRDS

Play the "picnic game" by going through the alphabet, from A to Z, and name an item you're going to bring on a picnic. For this game, pretend that you're going to a bird festival! ***(Extra challenge: make the items relate to birds if you can!)***

A ______

B ______

C ______

D ______

E ______

F ______

G ______

H ______

I ______

J ______

K ______

L ______

M ______

N ______

O ______

P ______

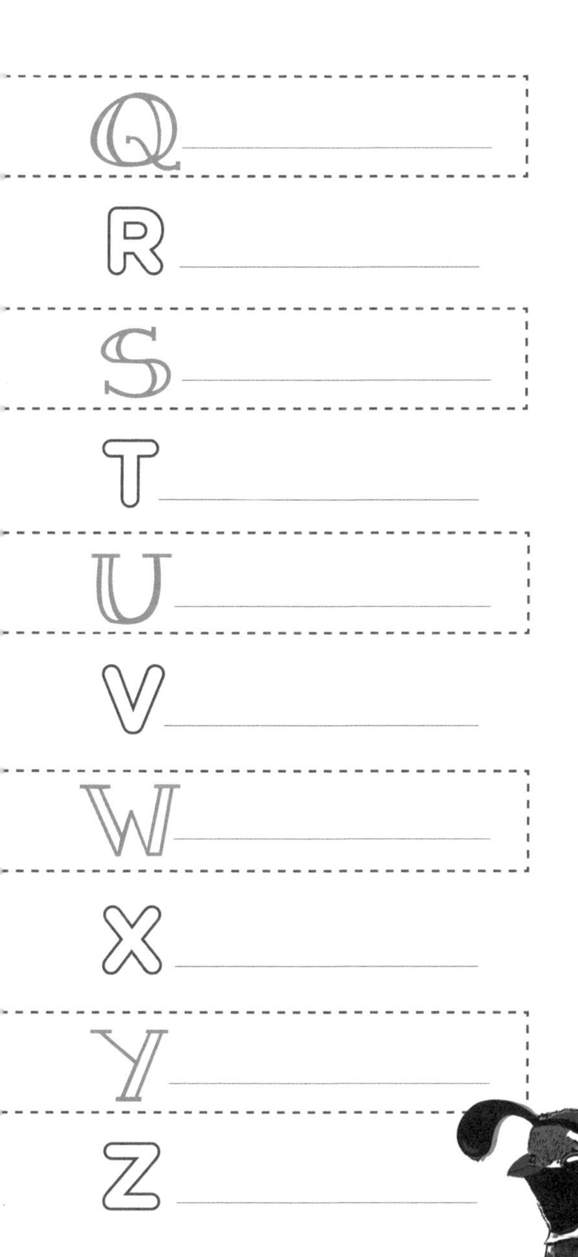

BIRD Facts

CALIFORNIA QUAILS

A California Quail's nest can have as many as 28 eggs in it! This is because females will often "dump" eggs in any nest they find nearby.

California Quails are found only in the West, but not just in California.

California Quail

FILL IN THE BIRD PHRASE

How well do you know bird phrases? Some of these are pretty old, so you may have to ask an adult for help. Good luck! *Answers are on page 95.*

The early bird gets the

______________________.

Get your ______________ in a row.

Your ________________ is cooked.

I will take you under my

______________________.

She's no ______________ chicken.

______________ duckling.

A little

____

told me.

Don't get your

____

ruffled.

The bird has flown

the ________________.

____

brain.

____

in your cap.

TheCornellLab

BIRD Facts

GREAT EGRETS

A Great Egret's nest can be up to 3 feet wide, and it can be up to 100 feet off the ground.

Great Egrets have a wingspan of almost 5 feet.

Great Egret

HISTORY LESSON

How well do you know your historical facts about birds? Test your knowledge here. Answers are found on page 95.

1. The Bald Eagle is the national bird right now, but what bird was almost selected in the 1700s?

A American Robin
B Wild Turkey
C Red-Tailed Hawk
D American Goldfinch

2. Which non-native bird was released in America in the 1800s and is now widespread across the continent?

A House Sparrow
B European Goldfinch
C Bullock's Oriole
D Mourning Dove

3. Which birds were in danger in the 1970s, but made a comeback after people starting putting up nest boxes?

A Cardinals B Wrens C Bluebirds D Blackbirds

4. Which of these is NOT a famous birder and ornithologist?

A John James Audubon
B Roger Tory Peterson
C Alexander Wilson
D John Muir

5. The last state to designate an official bird was Arizona in 1973. What is Arizona's state bird?

A Elf Owl
B Greater Roadrunner
C Vermilion Flycatcher
D Cactus Wren

6. Which of these birds are extinct?

A Carolina Parakeet
B Dodo
C Labrador Duck
D Great Auk
E All of the above

7. Martha is believed to be the world's last Passenger Pigeon. When did she die, making these birds extinct?

A 1850
B 1914
C 1975
D 1788

8. The selection of state birds began in 1927, and some of the first states to select birds included Florida, Wyoming, Maine, Alabama, Oregon, and Missouri. What is the state bird of Wyoming?

A Western Tanager
B Western Meadowlark
C Western Bluebird
D Western Scrub-Jay

BIRD Facts

WILD TURKEYS

Turkeys don't really fly well, right? Not so! Turkeys might not fly that much, but they can. They can even reach speeds up to 40 or 50 miles per hour.

At night, turkeys will often fly up into trees to roost.

Thanks to relocation efforts, Wild Turkeys can be found in every state except Alaska.

Wild Turkey

HOW WELL DO YOU KNOW THE BIRDS OF NORTH AMERICA?

Read the clues below, and see if you can guess which bird we are talking about. If you can guess the bird after only one or two clues, then you're doing really well! *Answers are on page 95.*

- I nest underground.
- I have long legs.
- I'm in the owl family.

WHAT BIRD AM I?

____

- I can mimic other birds.
- I am very smart.
- I have a crest.

WHAT BIRD AM I?

____

- I show up in summer.
- You can find several species, both in the East and West.
- I am known to eat oranges, and I build woven nests hanging near the ends of tree branches.

WHAT BIRD AM I?

____

- I'm only found in warm areas.
- I have a ring around my eye.
- Some people say I look like splashes of paint.

WHAT BIRD AM I? ______________________

- I am not a duck.
- I'm found in northern areas in summer.
- I dive deep into the water for fish.

WHAT BIRD AM I? ______________________

- I change colors in winter.
- Males are brighter than females.
- I like thistle seed.

WHAT BIRD AM I?

____

BIRD Facts

BLUE JAYS

Not all Blue Jays migrate, but when they do, they often fly by the hundreds. They also migrate during the day, which is rare for songbirds.

These birds often mimic the calls of hawks.

Blue Jay

EXPERIMENT

HOLD YOUR OWN

Bird Count

*You can participate in many great bird-watching programs like **Project FeederWatch** or the **Great Backyard Bird Count.** But first, practice up by holding your own bird count and submitting your results through **eBird.** Here are 5 tips to get you started.*

Get familiar with eBird

Get familiar with eBird by visiting eBird.org or downloading the eBird app. With eBird, you can record your bird sightings and make them available for scientists and other bird watchers to use.

How many bird species do you think you can see in 15 minutes?

Consider writing them down and entering a checklist in eBird. (You'll need to register an account, so ask your parents.)

____

Explore data

Look around on eBird.org to explore the data. For example, look up the birds that have recently been reported in your state. Which birds in my state do I want to see?

____

Sign up for a special event

Both Project FeederWatch (feederwatch.org) and the Great Backyard Bird Count (birdcount.org) are excellent options. Which count do you want to do and why?

____

____

Gather up friends

Birding is more fun when you get others involved. Put together some friends and make a little party of it.

The friends I would pick to join me:

____

____

____

5

Take photos

It's fun to observe the birds, but try taking a photo and uploading it on eBird, too. You could also record a sound with a phone or tablet.

What birds do I want to photograph?

____

____

____

The Cornell Lab

BIRD Facts

ATLANTIC PUFFINS

The Atlantic Puffin has earned the nickname "sea parrot" because of its large bill.

The two other puffins that live in the West include the Horned Puffin and Tufted Puffin.

Atlantic Puffin

HOW WELL DO YOU KNOW YOUR BIRDS?

You have to be honest when you take this quiz! Notice that you get an extra point if you've seen it, too! Write down a score for each bird in the list, then add your score up at the end.

1 **Huh? A what?**

2 **Sounds vaguely familiar.**

3 **Yes, I know that bird.**

4 **I know it, and I've seen one!**

Northern Shrike: _____

American Goldfinch: _____

Green Jay: _____

Canada Warbler: _____

Bobolink: _____

Lucifer Hummingbird: _____

Scissor-tailed Flycatcher: _____

Common Loon: _____

Bald Eagle: _____

Willow Ptarmigan: ____

Acorn Woodpecker: ____

50+ points: Wow! You both know and have seen a lot of birds.

40-50 points: Great work. Now start traveling to see more of them.

30-40 points: Not bad, but you have some work to do.

Under 30 points: Go outside right now and start seeing more birds.

BIRD Facts

AMERICAN GOLDFINCHES

The American Goldfinch is the state bird of New Jersey, Iowa, and Washington.

Even though females are lighter in color, you can still identify them with their distinct wingbars.

American Goldfinch

WOULD YOU RATHER...?

This "Would You Rather" game challenges you to decide which of two great birding moments you'd prefer to see! Just circle your favorite option.

Great Blue Heron eating a fish

Green Heron hunched in a tree?

Scarlet Tanager perched in your backyard

Western Tanager at your feeder?

Tufted Titmice at your sunflowers

Black-capped Chickadees on your coneflowers?

Snowy Owl flying in a field

Great Horned Owl roosting?

A soaring Bald Eagle

soaring Sandhill Cranes?

A nesting family of bluebirds

a nesting family of woodpeckers?

A young hummingbird learning to fly

a young hawk learning to fly?

Common Raven eating roadkill

a Turkey Vulture eating roadkill?

BIRD Facts

GREAT BLUE HERONS

Great Blue Herons tuck in their necks when they fly.

Herons don't weigh that much because, like most birds, they have hollow bones.

Great Blue Heron

MATCH THE MASCOT

You can find lots of examples of pro sports teams that have a bird as their official mascot. How well can you match them up? Draw a line from each city to the right mascot.
Answers are on page 96.

PITTSBURGH	ORIOLES
BALTIMORE	BLUE JAYS
TORONTO	CARDINALS
ST. LOUIS	PENGUINS
ARIZONA	SEAHAWKS
SEATTLE	CARDINALS

PELICANS

ATLANTA

FALCONS

NEW ORLEANS

EAGLES

ATLANTA

HAWKS

PHILADELPHIA

TheCornellLab

BIRD Facts

NORTHERN CARDINALS

Both the male and female Northern Cardinal help build the nest.

Sometimes a male cardinal will offer a seed to a female as part of courtship.

Northern Cardinal

GROWING UP BIRD

Be proud of your birding roots. Keep track of who got you started in birding right here so you can always remember them.

Who introduced you to birds? ____________________

What's one of the first memories you have of birding?

____

List all the people in your family who like birds:

____

FAMILY MEMBER: ____________________

FAVORITE BIRD: ____________________

FAMILY MEMBER: ____________________

FAVORITE BIRD: ____________________

FAMILY MEMBER: ____________________

FAVORITE BIRD: ____________________

FAMILY MEMBER: ____________________

FAVORITE BIRD: ____________________

FAMILY MEMBER: ____________________

FAVORITE BIRD: ____________________

FAMILY MEMBER: ____________________

FAVORITE BIRD: ____________________

If you know any famous birders, write about them here:

What was one of the first birds you liked as a little kid?

Where do you and your family go birding?

Do you and your family feed birds? If so, what are you favorite backyard birds?

Have you gone to any cool places for birding? List them here:

What are some of the places you want to go birding as a family?

Who have you inspired to become a birder?

BIRD Facts

AMERICAN ROBINS

American Robins are one of the first birds to sing in the morning and one of the last birds to sing at night.

Some birds hop while others run. Robins are runners.

While male and female American Robins look the same, there is one small difference. Females are just a little lighter in color than the males.

American Robin

ARE YOU A BIRD NERD?

How big of a "bird nerd" are you? If you aren't already a big bird nerd, we encourage you to keep trying. It's a great honor! Pick one answer for each question and find out on page 96!

If you hear about a cool or unusual bird in your area, what do you do?

A: Stop everything you're doing and go to find it.

B: Try to see it if you can.

C: Forget about it before you get a chance to see it.

How much would you say you know about birds?

A: More than most adults.

B: More than the average kid.

C: Not that much, but you like them.

Do you have a favorite bird?

A: Yes, but you also have like 10 runner-ups.

B: Sorta. You're still thinking about it.

C: Not really.

How often do you feed the birds?

A: All the time.

B: Sometimes.

C: Hardly ever.

What's your favorite time of year to go birding?

A: Obviously every season has its perks.

B: Whenever it's warm or nice out.

C: You don't go that often, so you don't really notice.

Do your friends know how much you love birds?

A: Yes, they've known for years.

B: Not really. I don't talk about it much.

C: Nah, it's not that big of a deal.

BIRD Facts

CHICKADEES

Chickadees can cache hundreds of seeds in a single day.

The oldest known chickadee living in the wild was 12 years and 5 months.

Black-capped Chickadee

WHAT BEAK IS THAT?

How many beaks can you match to the right birds? Draw a line from each beak to the bird to which you think it belongs. *Answers are on page 96.*

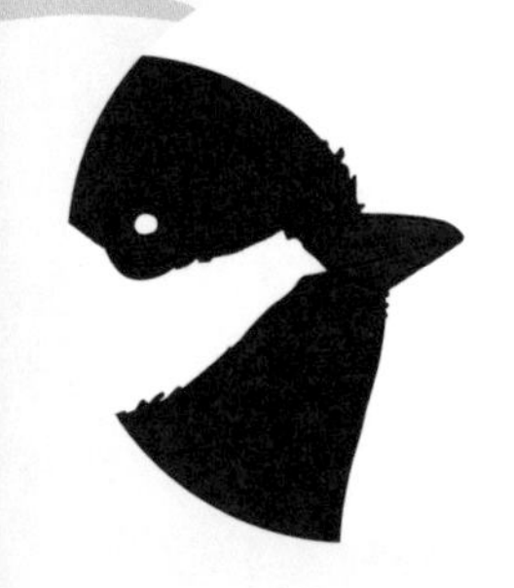

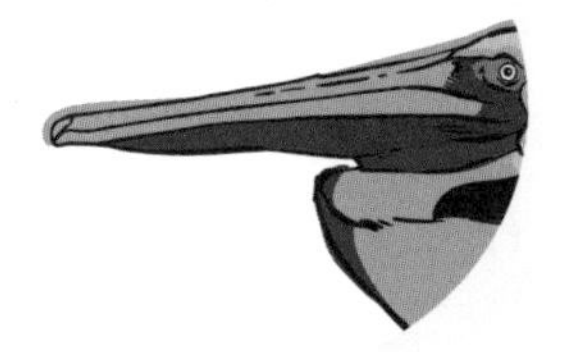

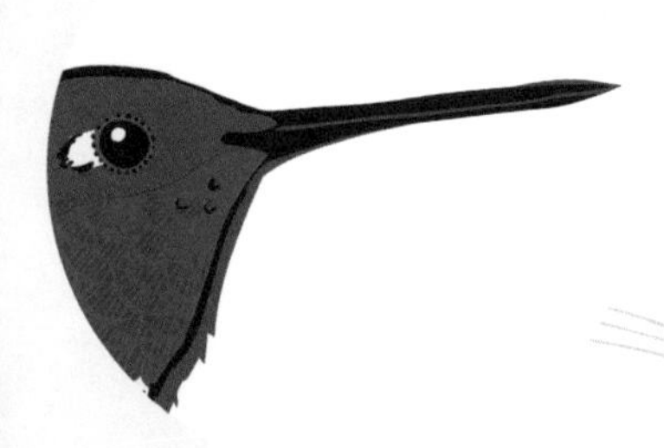

Blue Jay
Bald Eagle
Brown Pelican
Rufous Hummingbird
Black-capped Chickadee
Northern Cardinal

Wood Duck
Trumpeter Swan
Atlantic Puffin
Green Jay
Roseate Spoonbill
Northern Shrike

TheCornellLab

BIRD Facts

NORTHERN SHRIKES

Both male and female Northern Shrikes will sing throughout the year.

After the Northern Shrike kills its prey, eats it, and feeds it to its young, it will then sometimes store excess food for later by impaling it on thorns or barbed wire fences.

Northern Shrike

EXTREME BIRDS OF NORTH AMERICA

Can you guess the right bird for each fact below? Write it in, and then check how well you did with the answers on page 97. (Remember, these are for birds only found in North America.)

WHAT'S THE SMALLEST BIRD?

____

WHAT BIRD HAS THE MOST FEATHERS?

____

WHAT BIRD HAS THE LARGEST WINGSPAN?

____

WHAT'S THE FASTEST BIRD?

____

WHAT'S THE HEAVIEST OWL?

____

WHAT BIRD HAS THE LONGEST MIGRATION?

____

WHAT BIRD HAS THE BIGGEST NEST?

____

OTHER COOL FACTS ABOUT MY FAVORITE BIRDS:

____

____

____

TheCornellLab

BIRD Facts

PEREGRINE FALCONS

Like many in the falcon family, male Peregrine Falcons are smaller than females.

You can sometimes spot Peregrine Falcons in cities. They will nest on the ledges of water towers, bridges, or even skyscrapers.

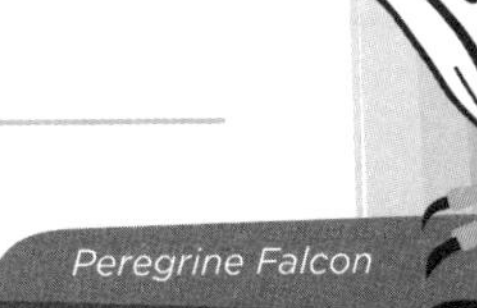
Peregrine Falcon

TRY A mini bioblitz

During a bioblitz, you try to document as many species and living things as you can in a set amount of time. They often last 24 hours, but try doing yours in just a few hours!

3 Facts About a Bioblitz

1 The first bioblitz was held in Washington, D.C., in 1996. The phrase came from Susan Rudy, a U.S. National Park Service naturalist.

2 What counts in a bioblitz? Pretty much any living thing, including plants.

3 Here's a good hint for doing a bioblitz—don't overlook anything. Even the small things count!

Here are the species we saw during the first 15 minutes:

Birds: ____________________

____

Invertebrates: ____________________

____

Other animals: ____________________

____

Plants: ____________________

____

Here are the species we saw between 15 minutes and 1 hour:

Birds: ______________________________

Invertebrates: ______________________

Other animals: ______________________

Plants: _____________________________

Here are the species we saw between 1 hour and 2 hours:

Birds: ______________________________

Invertebrates: ______________________

Other animals: ______________________

Plants: _____________________________

Here are the species we saw between 2 and 3 hours:

Birds: ______________________________

Invertebrates: ______________________

____

Other animals: ______________

____

Plants: _____________________________

The Cornell Lab

FUN Facts

MONARCHS

Monarchs need milkweed as a host plant in order to survive.

You can distinguish a male monarch from a female by a black scent gland on the hindwing.

Monarch caterpillars shed their skin about four times before turning into a butterfly.

WARBLER SCRAMBLE

Unscramble the following words to identify the various warblers. Find the answers on page 97.

ucblinranabk _ _ _ _ _ _ _ _ _ _ _ _ _ _

olwley _ _ _ _ _ _ _

oalpclbkl _ _ _ _ _ _ _ _ _ _ _

leub-wegndi _ _ _ _ _ _ _ _ _ _ _ _ _ _

erneluac _ _ _ _ _ _ _ _ _ _

etictucnocn _ _ _ _ _ _ _ _ _ _ _ _ _ _

cnaada _ _ _ _ _ _ _

anllsivhe _ _ _ _ _ _ _ _ _ _ _

dehdoo

_ _ _ _ _ _

kkeyutcn

_ _ _ _ _ _ _ _

maoilgna

_ _ _ _ _ _ _ _

viroednb

_ _ _ _ _ _ _ _

ownlis's

_ _ _ _ _ _ _ _

albkc-dna-hiwet

_ _ _ _ _ _ _ _ _ _ _ _ _ _ _ _ _ _ _ _

BIRD Facts

BLACKBURNIAN WARBLERS

The Blackburnian Warbler is the only warbler in North America with an orange throat.

After the young leave the nest, Blackburnian Warblers will sometimes forage with flocks of other birds including chickadees, nuthatches, and kinglets.

Blackburnian Warbler

TEST YOUR KNOWLEDGE

HOW WELL DO YOU KNOW YOUR STATE BIRDS?

This one is tricky! Match each bird listed to each state listed. Can you figure them all out? Answers are on page 97.

LOUISIANA

HAWAII

ARIZONA

NEW MEXICO

Greater Roadrunner | Ruffed Grouse | Common Loon | Brown Pelican

PENNSYLVANIA

MINNESOTA

NEW HAMPSHIRE

IDAHO

Nene | Cactus Wren | Mountain Bluebird | Purple Finch

TheCornellLab

BIRD Facts

WESTERN MEADOWLARKS & SCISSOR-TAILED FLYCATCHERS

The Western Meadowlark is the state bird for six states, including Montana, Kansas, Nebraska, North Dakota, Oregon, and Wyoming.

The Scissor-tailed Flycatcher is the state bird of just one state--Oklahoma.

Scissor-tailed Flycatcher

Western Meadowlark

BIRD LOG

BIRD:	
DATE:	
TIME:	
LOCATION:	
DETAILS:	

BIRD:	
DATE:	
TIME:	
LOCATION:	
DETAILS:	

BIRD:	
DATE:	
TIME:	
LOCATION:	
DETAILS:	

BIRD:	
DATE:	
TIME:	
LOCATION:	
DETAILS:	

BIRD:	
DATE:	
TIME:	
LOCATION:	
DETAILS:	

BIRD:	
DATE:	
TIME:	
LOCATION:	
DETAILS:	

BIRD LOG

BIRD:	
DATE:	
TIME:	
LOCATION:	
DETAILS:	

BIRD:	
DATE:	
TIME:	
LOCATION:	
DETAILS:	

BIRD:	
DATE:	
TIME:	
LOCATION:	
DETAILS:	

BIRD:	
DATE:	
TIME:	
LOCATION:	
DETAILS:	

BIRD:	
DATE:	
TIME:	
LOCATION:	
DETAILS:	

BIRD:	
DATE:	
TIME:	
LOCATION:	
DETAILS:	

BIRD LOG

BIRD:	
DATE:	
TIME:	
LOCATION:	
DETAILS:	

BIRD:	
DATE:	
TIME:	
LOCATION:	
DETAILS:	

BIRD:	
DATE:	
TIME:	
LOCATION:	
DETAILS:	

BIRD:	
DATE:	
TIME:	
LOCATION:	
DETAILS:	

BIRD:	
DATE:	
TIME:	
LOCATION:	
DETAILS:	

BIRD:	
DATE:	
TIME:	
LOCATION:	
DETAILS:	

BIRD LOG

BIRD:	
DATE:	
TIME:	
LOCATION:	
DETAILS:	

BIRD:	
DATE:	
TIME:	
LOCATION:	
DETAILS:	

BIRD:	
DATE:	
TIME:	
LOCATION:	
DETAILS:	

BIRD:	
DATE:	
TIME:	
LOCATION:	
DETAILS:	

BIRD:	
DATE:	
TIME:	
LOCATION:	
DETAILS:	

BIRD:	
DATE:	
TIME:	
LOCATION:	
DETAILS:	

BIRD LOG

BIRD:	
DATE:	
TIME:	
LOCATION:	
DETAILS:	

BIRD:	
DATE:	
TIME:	
LOCATION:	
DETAILS:	

BIRD:	
DATE:	
TIME:	
LOCATION:	
DETAILS:	

BIRD:	
DATE:	
TIME:	
LOCATION:	
DETAILS:	

BIRD:	
DATE:	
TIME:	
LOCATION:	
DETAILS:	

BIRD:	
DATE:	
TIME:	
LOCATION:	
DETAILS:	

BIRD LOG

BIRD:	
DATE:	
TIME:	
LOCATION:	
DETAILS:	

BIRD:	
DATE:	
TIME:	
LOCATION:	
DETAILS:	

BIRD:	
DATE:	
TIME:	
LOCATION:	
DETAILS:	

BIRD:	
DATE:	
TIME:	
LOCATION:	
DETAILS:	

BIRD:	
DATE:	
TIME:	
LOCATION:	
DETAILS:	

BIRD:	
DATE:	
TIME:	
LOCATION:	
DETAILS:	

BIRD LOG

BIRD:	
DATE:	
TIME:	
LOCATION:	
DETAILS:	

BIRD:	
DATE:	
TIME:	
LOCATION:	
DETAILS:	

BIRD:	
DATE:	
TIME:	
LOCATION:	
DETAILS:	

BIRD:	
DATE:	
TIME:	
LOCATION:	
DETAILS:	

BIRD:	
DATE:	
TIME:	
LOCATION:	
DETAILS:	

BIRD:	
DATE:	
TIME:	
LOCATION:	
DETAILS:	

BIRD LOG

BIRD:	
DATE:	
TIME:	
LOCATION:	
DETAILS:	

BIRD:	
DATE:	
TIME:	
LOCATION:	
DETAILS:	

BIRD:	
DATE:	
TIME:	
LOCATION:	
DETAILS:	

BIRD:	
DATE:	
TIME:	
LOCATION:	
DETAILS:	

BIRD:	
DATE:	
TIME:	
LOCATION:	
DETAILS:	

BIRD:	
DATE:	
TIME:	
LOCATION:	
DETAILS:	

BIRD LOG

BIRD:	
DATE:	
TIME:	
LOCATION:	
DETAILS:	

BIRD:	
DATE:	
TIME:	
LOCATION:	
DETAILS:	

BIRD:	
DATE:	
TIME:	
LOCATION:	
DETAILS:	

BIRD:	
DATE:	
TIME:	
LOCATION:	
DETAILS:	

BIRD:	
DATE:	
TIME:	
LOCATION:	
DETAILS:	

BIRD:	
DATE:	
TIME:	
LOCATION:	
DETAILS:	

HOW TO DRAW BIRDS

Our illustrator, Rachel Riordan, offers some step-by-step instructions for drawing some common birds of North America. If you're an aspiring artist, practice as much as possible. You'll only get better and better!

How to draw a Sandhill Crane

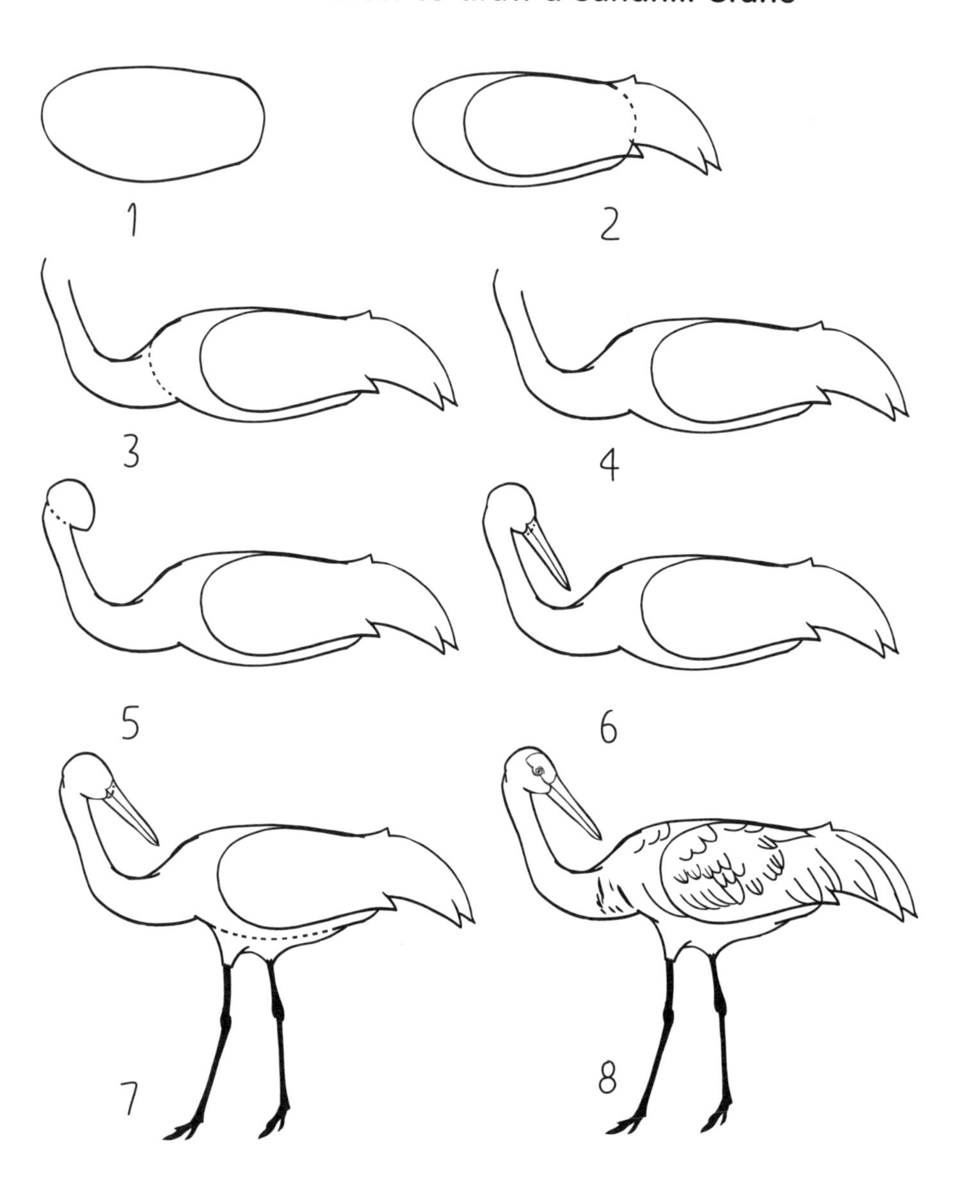

Draw a Sandhill Crane

How to draw an Atlantic Puffin

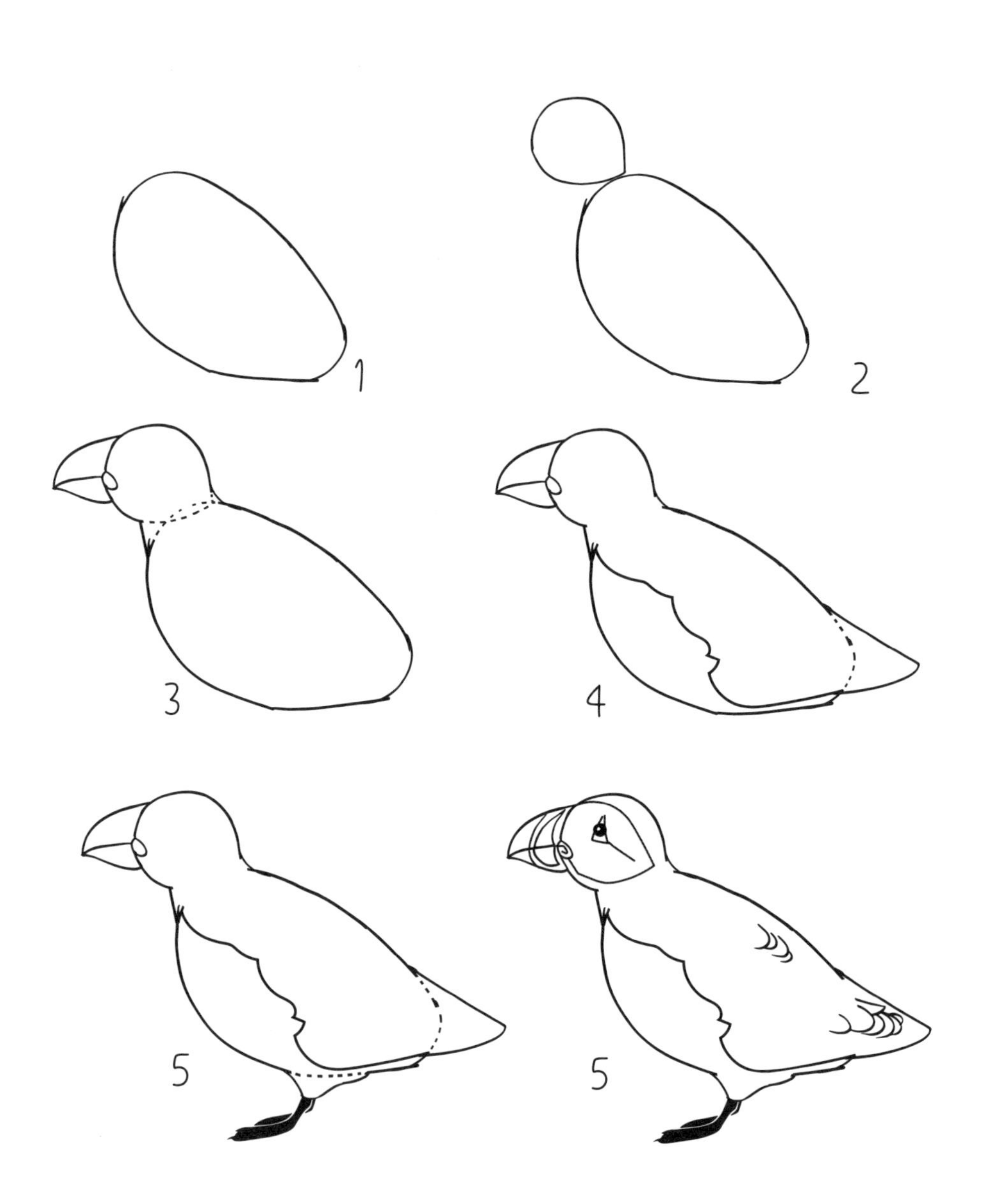

Draw an Atlantic Puffin

HOW TO DRAW BIRDS

How to draw a Green Jay

Draw a Green Jay

How to draw a Chickadee

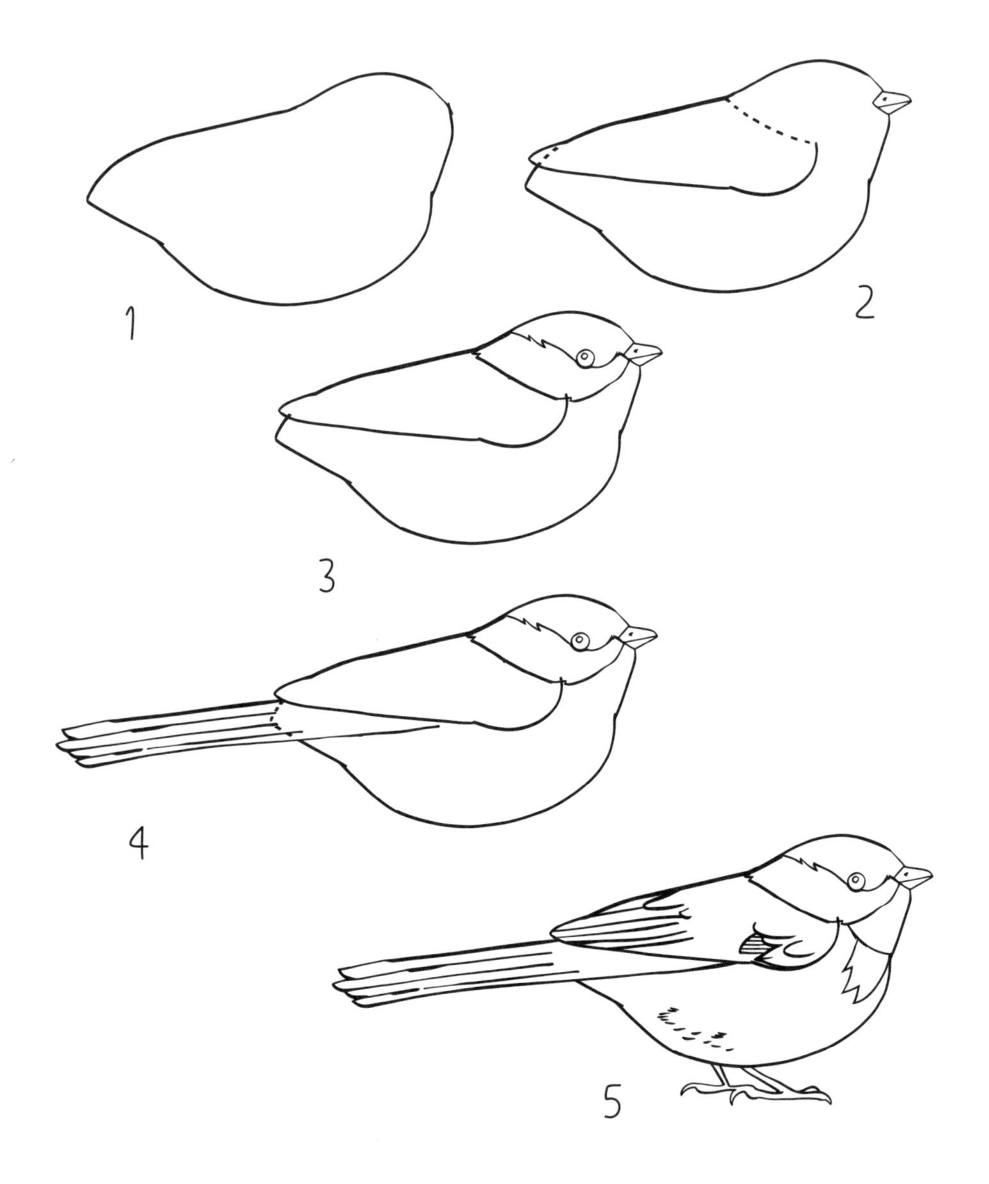

Draw a Chickadee

How to draw a Greater Roadrunner

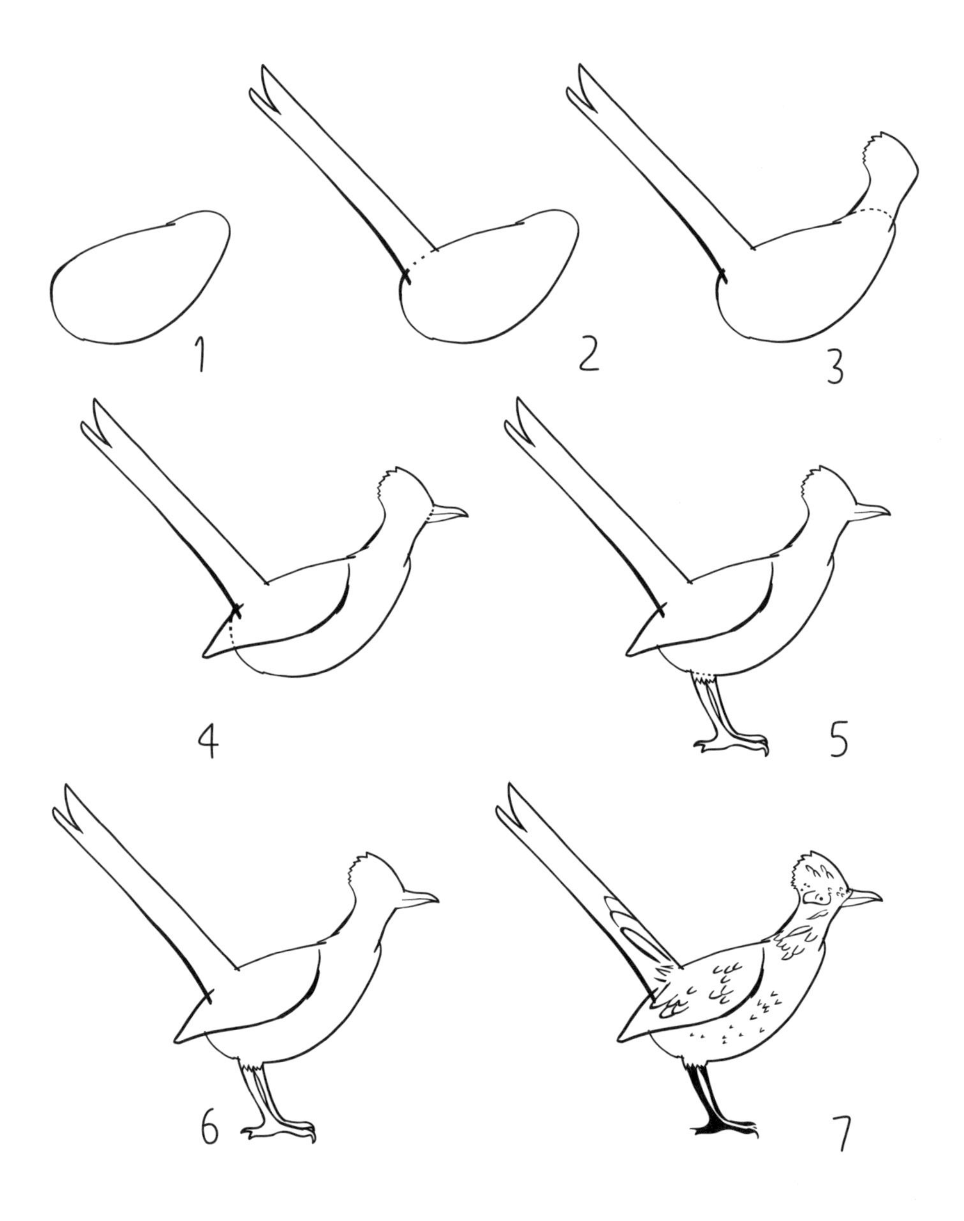

Draw a Greater Roadrunner

ABOUT THE CORNELL LAB OF ORNITHOLOGY

The Cornell Lab of Ornithology is a world leader in the study, appreciation, and conservation of birds. Here are five things you might not know about the Cornell Lab:

1. The Lab was founded in 1915. Today, it has its own beautiful building within a wooded sanctuary in Ithaca, New York.

2. Millions of people have fun learning about birds and birding through the Lab's popular websites including **allaboutbirds.org**.

3. You can actually visit the famous Cornell Lab and even go for a walk in Sapsucker Woods. Free guided walks are held every weekend!

4. The Cornell Lab is a leader in citizen science, which involves ordinary people helping scientists. Many of the programs have been mentioned in this book, but if you want to get involved, visit **birds.cornell.edu**.

5. The Cornell Lab is a member-based organization, so you can sign up for your very own membership, too. If you do, you'll get a copy of their magazine, *Living Bird* (**birds.cornell.edu/join**).

AND OUR PERSONAL FAVORITE
THE BIRD CAMS!

LIVE VIDEO STREAMING

Want to get up close and personal
with wild birds right now?

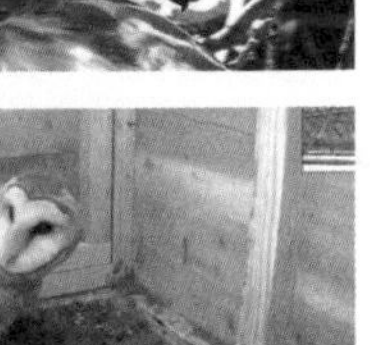

CAMS.ALLABOUTBIRDS.ORG

Visit the Lab's live bird cams
to catch all the action!

MORE BIRD ACTIVITIES FOR YOU TO EXPLORE

All About Birds
The Cornell Lab created this dynamic website so you can delve into everything you want to know about birds. See photos, listen to the bird songs, and learn little-known and interesting facts.
allaboutbirds.org

Cornell Lab Bird Academy
Try fun online activities that teach you about bird biology, including behavior and anatomy. You can also sign up for courses about bird identification, bird song, and other topics.
academy.allaboutbirds.org

Merlin Bird ID App
What's that bird? Merlin will ask you five easy questions to help you identify the birds you see.
merlin.allaboutbirds.org

Young Birders Network
This is an awesome website if you're looking to join a Young Birders Network club near you. It even has tips for starting your own club!
ebird.org/content/ybn

BirdSleuth
You can get your school interested in birds or just do some of the activities on your own.
birdsleuth.org

Bird Cams
You can learn so much about birds just by observing them. Check out the feeder and nest cams online.
cams.allaboutbirds.org

Celebrate Urban Birds
Lots of birds live in and around cities. Get involved in art and science projects involving urban birds.
celebrateurbanbirds.org

NestWatch
Help scientists learn more about birds by finding nests and sharing your data online.
nestwatch.org

eBird
Share your bird sightings in this worldwide citizen-science project. You can also explore the data to find out what birds other people are seeing in any area you choose.
ebird.org

ABA Young Birders
Check out the "Young Birder of the Year" awards and other news about events and opportunities.
youngbirders.aba.org

Junior Duck Stamp Conservation Program
If you're good at drawing and art, you'll want to consider entering this annual competition. Plus, it supports conservation efforts.
fws.gov/duckstamps

Macaulay Library
You can hear bird, whale, and other animal sounds from all over the world and watch some amazing videos on this website from the Cornell Lab.
macaulaylibrary.org

ANSWER KEY

From "HOW WELL DO YOU KNOW OWLS?"
Answers:
1. C, **2.** D, **3.** B, **4.** A, **5.** B, **6.** A, **7.** D, **8.** C

From "TWO TRUTHS AND A LIE"
Answers:
BIRD POOP: T, F, T; **DUCKS:** F, T, T; **FEEDING:** T, F, T; **CROWS:** T,F, T; **ORIOLES:** T, T, F; **WARBLERS:** F, T, T; **BIRDHOUSES:** T, F, T; **HUMMINGBIRDS:** T, T, F

From "WHAT'S FOR DINNER?"
Answers:
Greater Roadrunner = Snake
Rufous Hummingbird = Nectar
Great Horned Owl = Rabbit
Sandhill Crane = Plant Tubers
Western Bluebird = Mealworms
Turkey Vulture = Roadkill
Wild Turkey = Cracked Corn
Yellow Warbler = Gnats
Black-capped Chickadee = Black-oil Sunflower Seeds
Roseate Spoonbill = Shrimp

From "ARE YOU A NATURE PRO?"
Mostly As: Pro. You're a nature pro! Nothing intimidates you.
Mostly Bs: Amateur. You're working on becoming a pro and are trying to get over being timid.
Mostly Cs: Rookie. Don't give up! Maybe a pro can help you get over some fears.

From "BIRD MNEMONICS"

Answers:

Drink your tea = Eastern Towhee
Peter, Peter, Peter = Tufted Titmouse
Who cooks for you? = Barred Owl
Sweet, sweet, I'm so sweet = Yellow Warbler
Oh sweet Canada, Canada, Canada = White-throated Sparrow
Cheese bur-ger = Black-capped Chickadee
I gotta go wee wee right now = White-crowned Sparrow

From "FILL IN THE BIRD PHRASE"

Worm
Ducks
Goose
Wing
Spring
Ugly
Birdie
Feathers
Coop
Bird
Feather

From "HISTORY LESSON"

Answers:

1. B; **2.** A; **3.** C; **4.** D; **5.** D; **6.** E; **7.** B; **8.** B

From "HOW WELL DO YOU KNOW THE BIRDS OF NORTH AMERICA?"

Burrowing Owl
Blue Jay
Oriole
Painted Bunting
Common Loon
American Goldfinch

From "MATCH THE MASCOT"

Pittsburgh Penguins
Baltimore Orioles
Toronto Blue Jays
St. Louis Cardinals
Arizona Cardinals
Seattle Seahawks
Atlanta Falcons
New Orleans Pelicans
Atlanta Hawks
Philadelphia Eagles

From "ARE YOU A BIRD NERD?"

Mostly As: You are a total bird nerd. Wear the title proudly, and try to convert others!
Mostly Bs: You have a solid love for birds, but it can definitely get nerdier!
Mostly Cs: You are curious about birds. Let's increase that love even more!

From "WHAT BEAK IS THAT?"

 Blue Jay

 Bald Eagle

 Brown Pelican

 Rufous Hummingbird

 Black-capped Chickadee

 Northern Cardinal

 Wood Duck

 Trumpeter Swan

 Atlantic Puffin

 Green Jay

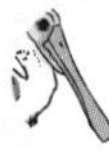 Roseate Spoonbill

 Northern Shrike